DANVI...
W9-AMA-628
3 1205 0037...

LESSONS
FROM A
Caregiver

PUBLIC LIBRARY
DANVILLE, ILLINOIS

LESSONS
FROM A
Caregiver

CARING FOR AN ELDER
WITH LOVE AND
COMPASSION

LAUREL A. WICKS

GIBBS SMITH
TO ENRICH AND INSPIRE HUMANKIND
Salt Lake City | Charleston | Santa Fe | Santa Barbara

First Edition
13 12 11 10 09   5 4 3 2 1

Text © 2009 Laurel A. Wicks

All rights reserved. No part of this book may be reproduced by any means whatsoever without written permission from the publisher, except brief portions quoted for purpose of review.

Published by
Gibbs Smith
P.O. Box 667
Layton, Utah 84041

1-800.835.4993 orders
www.gibbs-smith.com

Cover Design by Sheryl Dickert
Interior Design by mGraphicDesign
Printed and bound in the United States
Gibbs Smith books are printed on either recycled, 100% post-consumer waste, FSC-certified papers or on paper produced from a 100% certified sustainable forest/controlled wood source.

Library of Congress Cataloging-in-Publication Data

Wicks, Laurel A.
  Lessons from a caregiver : caring for an elder with love and compassion / Laurel A. Wicks. — 1st ed.
     p. cm.
  ISBN-13: 978-1-4236-0553-9
  ISBN-10: 1-4236-0553-5
  1. Older people—Care—Psychological aspects. 2. Compassion. 3. Older people—Health and hygiene. 4. Caregivers—Vocational guidance. I. Title.
  HV1451.W53 2009
  649.8084'6—dc22
                              2009003227

649.80846
WiC
cop.1

For Huck, my father, a wise, kind, and humble man
who taught me about living and dying nobly

PUBLIC LIBRARY
DANVILLE, ILLINOIS

Contents

Preface 9

Acknowledgments 14

1. "Being There" Is the Start 19

2. Living in the Household 27

3. Learning that Safety Is No Accident 45

4. Navigating Doctors, Insurance, and Finances 57

5. Devising Activities for Fun and Stimulation 69

6. Implementing Personal Care 81

7. Concentrating on Food, Eating, and Nutrition... 91

   —Casual Recipes.................................... 104

8. Caring for the Caregiver........................... 123

9. Accepting the Final Days and
   Carrying Out Final Wishes......................... 131

10. Contemplating the Future of Caregiving 139

Passing 146

Resources 149

Preface

~~~~~~~~~~~~~~~~~~~~~~~~~~~~~~~~~~~~~~

I came to elder caring through the kitchen door, with no inkling of what might lie ahead. I was hired to deliver a few meals to an elder by a family member. Having worked many years in a progression of culinary roles as a baker, pastry chef, restaurant owner, caterer, and food industry consultant, I had become a personal chef, providing the services of shopping, meal planning, and meal preparation for several households. Proceeding as usual, I interviewed the client about likes and dislikes and any specific dietary restrictions. It was agreed that I would deliver the meals just before noon two days each week.

The first day, I brought the meals and put them in the refrigerator. They were each labeled and dated, and they were either ready to eat or had instructions attached for heating or cooking.

Upon my return three days later, the meals were untouched. I asked if anything was wrong. "Oh, no," was the reply. This went on for two weeks. One day, I just decided to set the table, plate the meal, and make tea. I summoned my client, and then I sat and had tea while she ate. "That tasted really quite good," was the reply.

So it began. I'd set the table with lovely china and cloth napkins, and my client would eat and even talk a bit. I noticed the cat needed brushing. I sat on the floor and brushed the cat. When the meal was finished, I cleaned off the kitchen counters and loaded the dishwasher. The meals in the refrigerator started to disappear.

A few weeks later, my client fell, broke her arm, and was hospitalized. I made some cookies and went to the hospital to visit. There was a book on the bed table. I asked if she had read any of it yet. "No, it's too hard to hold the book."

I said, "I have a bit of time, I'll start it." Over protests that it wasn't possible to read a book out loud, I began.

As she lay quietly with eyes closed, I read a chapter. At the end of the chapter, I was sure that she was asleep, so

I quietly closed the book. With eyes still closed, her tiny voice said, "You read that beautifully. Would you go on?" So I read another chapter.

When she returned home with her arm in a sling, more help was needed. It was requested that I spend more hours and help with dressing, meals, driving to appointments, and household chores. There was always time for more reading. We finished our first book.

As time went on here in this small town, the family doctor took note that even as my client moved toward the end of her life, there was improvement in her quality of life. I began to get phone calls. The family doctor and the head of the oncology department sent referrals my way. People began asking me questions about what I did or how I handled common situations. There were lots of job offers.

And so it went, and so it grew. If there is anything true about elder caring, it is that the needs become greater and more complex as time passes. There may be an escalation of tasks that involve scheduling twenty-four-hour care and household maintenance or making other difficult choices before life ends. And even then, there are wishes to be carried out and details to be settled. Sometimes the elder in need is alone. If family is close by, they are often preoccupied with aspects of their already busy lives. Someone needs to hold the center in a vortex of change.

These words explain the facts, but that's not really what is important. The crucial element is in the space between the words and the actions, where one allows oneself to open up in some way just to *be present* for another person. There was something in me that could see the needs of another and sought to meet them. I could sense a lonely place, and I would reach to fill it with compassion and cheer. It has now been more than eight years, and caring for elders has become my work and my joy.

I write to share my insights and to be of service to others. It's not that I want to tell anyone what to do, but my experiences may help others to see some steps on their own path. I invite you to be a fearless advocate for the elder or elders who need your help. I remind you to enjoy the unfolding moments of insight. I urge you to seek out the many rewarding experiences in elder caring. Although this is written about my caring for elders, those who care for a sick, injured, or

terminally ill person face most of the same issues. This is for
those who give care to those who need care.

I tend to sound Pollyanna-ish. My attitude is to
remain as cheerful and positive as possible. This does not
mean that I am not fully aware that the aging process is
anything but the winding down of a precious life. I know
that. I have been intimately present during this time of
diminishing that leads to the letting go of a life that once
sparked the spirit and body of a beloved. What does it
mean to be present for someone who no longer knows who
I am? How does it feel to care for the baffled, unaware,
incontinent one who once so relished lively conversations of deep thought? How is it possible to listen to the
last breath, and then clean up and go on?

It is. It just is. I sign up to comfort, nourish, and see
the person to the end of their days with as much dignity
and affection as possible. That is the unaltered truth.
The path of life goes on, showing us so much, if we are
willing to be open, renew ourselves, and be present as
each day unfolds.

—Laurel A. Wicks

Acknowledgments

My life and this book would be less without a little help from my friends and family. I want to express my gratitude to these people for gifts given and insights shared:

Valentino Littlewing, who reminds me again and again to be present, helping to open my heart every day

Blanche Chase, how mysterious that someone can always be three steps ahead of me and behind me all the way

Kat Miller, who gives me the gift of centering and grounding wisdom, who knew I needed to write this book before I knew

Liz Lockhart, for generosity and trust, starting me on a path

Jan Bauer, the wee Irish nurse, soothing presence to her patients, teacher to caregivers, student of dharma

Peg, my mother, always there with kind and gentle guidance

Lynn and Lee Donaldson, my brothers, and my nieces and nephews, Alicia, Eric, Carmen, and Lucas, who help create the web of care that holds our beloved matriarch

Dr. Bruce Hayse, a mentor and ally who provides timely and supportive answers with patience, intelligence, and a bit of lighthearted humor

Roberta, my shy friend with exquisite taste

Richard Charlesworth, for sharing from his heart

Diana Walter and the healing our yoga class brings

Brad and Kate Mead, Cliff and Martha Hansen, and their strong supporting family

The team of nurturing, attentive beings with whom
I work

All of the home health care and hospice nurses who have
been there with grace and skill when I needed them

The Jackson Hole Historical Society

The Senior Center of Jackson

❧

"*Oak trees just grow stronger*

Rivers grow wilder every day

Old people just grow lonesome

Waiting for someone to say

'Hello in there, hello.'"

~ John Prine,
from his debut album
John Prine

~~~~~~

" . . . YOU NEVER REALLY UNDERSTAND
A PERSON UNTIL YOU CONSIDER THINGS
FROM HIS POINT OF VIEW . . . UNTIL YOU
CLIMB INTO HIS SKIN AND WALK AROUND
IN IT . . ."

~ HARPER LEE,
FROM HER BOOK
To Kill a Mockingbird

~~~~~~

1

"Being There" Is the Start

For a caregiver, it's almost impossible to be with an elder without trying to imagine who and how this person used to be in their vitality of life. Was there once a mischievous sparkle in the eyes now dimmed? Was it a life of bold adventure or grand love? Gnarled, weathered hands might have meant a life of outdoor work, mending fences, birthing calves, nurturing the garden behind the house. Long delicate fingers could have played the piano that sits unnoticed with its tall stack of music in the darkened living room. It could have been a life of steadfast dedication to work and family, profound in the ordinary day to day. Now that person has aged and changed. And caregivers must bring all of the wisdom, compassion, patience, and understanding they can to *be present* for the person who is now before them.

This is the beginning of a relationship. Whether the person you are caring for is a new client, a stranger to you, or a relative you've always known, becoming a caregiver is a new beginning. Being in a position to *need* a caregiver is probably both new and shocking to the elder, and having a caregiver might not have been the elder's idea. Being kind will go a long way toward creating the environment you will share for the unforeseeable future.

Getting Started

This process begins before you might actually start caring for an elder. Whether it is a new client or someone you know, you must first center your emotional self and envision the possibilities of the future. If it is a family member who is in need or is going to need care in the future, then start the conversation now, before any untoward event occurs. Find out early on what the elder's wishes are. Be in touch with the physical, emotional, and financial realities. Talk about the fears and always be reassuring that you or someone will be there. It is important to be skillful and caring at the same time.

Take a census of emotions for each of you. How do you feel? How do you think the other person feels? What shows in body language? What can you share of yourself to put the other person at ease? Start a conversation where you are open to listen, really listen, to what the elder has to say.

When you first meet the elder, what do you notice immediately that might make the other person's world more comfortable and help them feel at ease? Do they have a pillow that needs plumping or does the bed need straightening? What compliment can you give about the room you are in or the person's home? Is there a favorite pet to befriend that might need special attention? Do the plants need watering? Could you offer a cup of tea or coffee? Sometimes it is good to be useful. Maybe it is more appropriate to ask about any specific matter needing attention that is on the elder's mind.

Tuning In

There are different kinds of relationships between caregivers and elders. If caregiving is your occupation, caring for an elder you have never met is always a fresh start. Caring for your own parent may carry a lot of baggage built up over decades. This can be extremely challenging, and it is the opportunity to do a deep internal inventory of clearing yourself of patterns of the past while working to stay in the present.

Being with one elder in need is much different from being with an elder married couple who has a history of relationship dynamics. It takes time to get to know each person, to relate to them as individuals, and to strike a balance between being in their household and respecting their privacy at the same time.

Showing Respect

It seems that elders become like children in some ways as their world becomes smaller. It is as if they distill to their original essence. They surely need delicate care, but it is not appropriate to treat them as inferiors or to talk down to them.

Imagine how it feels to lose the ability to make the choices, one by one, over aspects of your life. Allow the elder to be part of the decision-making process, even if it is about little things. It may help them retain some dignity.

Elders can be easily offended or get defensive. It's important to allow them not to be "wrong." Let's say you are reading the newspaper out loud to someone still interested in keeping up with events but whose eyes aren't capable of reading any more. While you are reading, the person dozes off. You stop reading, and moments later the person comes back to consciousness and asks why you stopped reading. If you say, "You fell asleep," chances are the person will get defensive. If you say, "My throat is a little tired. Why don't you rest while I do a few chores? We'll finish reading later. Would that be okay?" it allows the person not to be wrong. That interaction keeps the elder from feeling or being inadequate. Asking instead of telling allows the elder to be a part of the decision process.

DEALING WITH EXPANDING NEEDS

Elder care can be like floodwaters in that their needs expand to fill all space and time. Figuring out realistically how to deal with timing is huge. Remembering that it now takes an hour instead of twenty minutes to be ready to leave for an appointment can relieve a lot of stress. The process of elder caring is one of escalation as the person's condition declines and personal needs increase. Change is the constant. You may notice that just when things seem in balance and there is time to take a deep breath and relax a little, something new develops. Once again it is time to figure out a new solution to help life flow smoothly.

Taking care of an elder involves using a thousand little ways to frame situations to make life more palatable for everyone. Being flexible and keeping a sense of humor may be the most important skills to have. Being kind, thoughtful, and caring are always appropriate.

❦

NOTES

"... THE DECEMBER SNOW FELL
QUIETLY WITHOUT, AND THE FIRE
CRACKLED CHEERFULLY WITHIN. IT WAS A
COMFORTABLE OLD ROOM, THOUGH THE
CARPET WAS FADED AND THE FURNITURE
VERY PLAIN, FOR A GOOD PICTURE OR
TWO HUNG ON THE WALLS, BOOKS FILLED
THE RECESSES, CHRYSANTHEMUMS AND
CHRISTMAS ROSES BLOOMED IN THE
WINDOWS, AND A PLEASANT ATMOSPHERE
OF HOME-PEACE PERVADED IT."

~ LOUISA MAY ALCOTT,
FROM HER BOOK
Little Women

2

Living in the Household

People have many deep feelings about home. Dorothy in *The Wizard of Oz* was right when she clicked her ruby slippers together and said, "There's no place like home." All the old clichés are true. Home is where the heart is. A person's home is his castle. It is vitally important to an elderly person's well-being that his home is cared for in a loving and respectful manner, as it is an extension of his personality.

There are folks who are always clean and tidy. They will clean their home before going on a trip. They will clean even when they are ill. They will look around and, if things don't look right, they will be compelled to get up and put things in a certain order before they feel good enough to get well. What we see before us can be either soothing or unsettling to our psyche. Oftentimes elders become more agitated as their health declines. Keeping their surroundings orderly, even beautiful—or at least free of chaos—helps them to remain calm. It's probably true for caregivers and family members, too.

The elder with whom you are charged is the center of the whole functioning entity of a household. Being with the elder, spending time directly focused on the person, talking, and reading is vitally important when that person needs and wants attention. The elder is the reason you are there. However, there is always time when the elder is otherwise occupied that attention can be given to the home. If the elder wants to, plans to, or is capable of staying in her home, then the household operation will need to run smoothly. As time goes on, there is a probability that the household could have caregivers twenty-four hours a day for seven days a week. This takes organization and planning, and it will be a cumulative effort.

DETAILING A LOG BOOK

A log book is essential. It is so easy to forget when things happened. As an elder's care becomes more complex, more people will become involved. Everyone in attendance needs to sign in and out with date, times, and the specifics of their shift. Caregivers must contribute to the daily log, and they are also responsible for reading through everyone else's entries, from their own last entry to the current one, to make sure they don't miss an update on any pertinent issues. Entries might be about medications, developing care complexities, or perhaps something as mundane as the veterinarian said not to let the cat out for 48 hours.

Perhaps at a doctor's visit there was discussion of a mild symptom that had developed. The doctor will ask when it was first noticed. There it is in the dated and signed notes.

Elders with memory loss might be anxious about some detail of yesterday, like a friend calling. If you weren't there but you have read the notes, you can say, "Emily called you yesterday. You had a lovely visit and talked about her granddaughter's wedding." That sort of reassurance is helpful. Visits and calls from family and friends are important to note. Many elders need to be

PUBLIC LIBRARY
DANVILLE, ILLINOIS

reassured that they have not been forgotten; family and friends are able to comment on the visits of others.

> *"Emily called you yesterday. You had a lovely visit and talked about her granddaughter's wedding."*

Not nearly as much fun, but important nonetheless, are the details about eating or not, amount of liquids consumed, and bowel movements.

Usually, writing narrative style in the logbook is just fine. It is more important to be complete. It is not about being self-conscious regarding your abilities in spelling, grammar, or sentence structure. Getting the information down in writing is what is helpful to the elder's care. If there has been an incident that necessitated a doctor's visit, then a chart may be set up for medications that enter the household, noting what time and in what amounts medications are dispensed, with all caregivers initialing the chart when meds are given.

10-21-2008: Oxycodone—20 pills from pharmacy—One to be given with food every six hours for pain

10-21-2008: Swiss Kriss laxative—24 tablets—One to be given with each pain pill to prevent constipation

	8AM	2PM	8PM	2AM
10-21 OXY	LAW	LAW	SD	SD
10-21 SKLAX	LAW	LAW	SD	SD
10-22 OXY	LAW	LAW	JCD	SD
10-22 SKLAX	LAW	LAW	JCD	SD

KEEPING A CALENDAR

Having a household calendar is really important. Use it to record birthdays, anniversaries, appointments outside the home, car registration, or when the taxes are due, as well as scheduling caregivers. It doesn't matter what the detail is, it's more likely to be handled on time if it's noted in black-and-white on the central calendar.

It allows whoever is in charge to see at a glance what needs to be handled that day.

Most elders like to commemorate family birthdays. You might need to research the dates, transfer them onto a new calendar each year, remind the elder well in advance so you can help them choose presents or select cards, and then get them mailed on time. This singular detail can be extremely important to your elder's feeling of well-being.

Making a Chore List

A list of chores is a useful tool. There can be a lot of frustration accumulated when details are not handled, so it is important that everyone involved knows who is to do what and when. Put the lists on a computer and update as needed. Give a copy of all household-related material to each caregiver involved. Keep one in a central location. The side of the refrigerator is a universally known spot. When anyone new enters the household, there is much to share. It's minutiae, undoubtedly, but if it is all written in the lists, then there is no argument, and there is a place for the buck to stop. Make a list of morning chores, evening chores, weekly, monthly, and those that pertain to the personal and medical care of the elder and the household. Include doing the laundry, cleaning the bathroom, dusting, rotating foods, cleaning out the refrigerator, emptying the cat box—whatever needs to be done. Here are some examples:

- Trash day—every Monday except holidays, and then it is picked up on Tuesday. Take the can to the curb before 8 a.m.
- Hair appointment—Every Friday at 10:30 a.m. Call ahead if you won't make it.
- Oxygen delivery—Every Tuesday, usually morning.
- Plant feeding—Second Thursday of the month. The food is in the left cupboard under the kitchen sink. Use a 1 to 4 ratio.
- Foot clinic—Third Wednesday of each month at the Senior Center at 12:30. Get there early to avoid a long wait.

POSTING PHONE NUMBERS

Keeping a list of all important phone numbers is really handy. Post it on the refrigerator with other important papers. The list includes medical professionals, the hospital, relatives, friends, caregivers, haircutter, veterinarian, plumber, electrician, and everyone important to the household. Make sure those involved know who is in charge of each particular decision that needs to be made and make a note by the contact information. If the elder can recall who is usually hired or contacted for such things, all the better. If not, seek advice from family members or whoever hired you.

Accountant

Attorney

Air conditioner/furnace

Beauty salon/barbershop

Caregivers 1, 2, 3, 4 . . .

   (and their current schedules)

Dentist

Doctors

Electrician

Family

Gardener

Lawn care

Mechanic

Pastor

Plumber

RECYCLING AND GREENING

The greening of households may not be of interest to all, but it is the way of the future, and it is required in some parts of the country. Have a conversation of understanding with your elder first and make sure it is fine with them before you embark on a household greening or recycling project. It's really easy to set up a few plastic tubs or cardboard boxes with appropriate labels, out of sight of the elder, in the basement, in a closet, in the garage, or under the stairs. Be sure that you remain responsible and take it to the drop-off often. You may choose to take the recycling home when you leave each day. It's amazing how much trash can be averted.

You might also consider switching to cleaning products that are earth friendly. These less toxic products are gentler for the delicate systems of elders. Often in elders' houses there is considerable trash created by necessities such as diapers, plastic sheets, and latex gloves. Though these modern-day products are a blessing, they do have an impact. Using biodegradable trash bags, switching to more efficient lightbulbs, and lightening the trash load

LIVING IN THE HOUSEHOLD

by recycling can help give a sense of balance.

ORGANIZING "STUFF"

Some people have a tendency to collect "stuff." Sometimes it's good, and sometimes it just leads to disorganized clutter. Organizing things with your elder can be a fun project. A hall or bedroom closet might be an obvious place to start. Talk about the project with your elder first so that they are aware that you won't get rid of things without permission. You will undoubtedly find some treasures that make for good conversation and reminiscence. Let the elder sit comfortably while you go through the items and put them into categories. Ask the elder about them. Some items may be earmarked for specific family members; others might be given to charities. Some items may lead to projects to do together.

CREATING COMFORT

Creating comfort in the surroundings of your elder will add to the ease and well-being. When there is an issue of memory loss, recognizable surroundings may be particularly important. If the person has a favorite color, then having a blanket or pillow or bouquet of that color nearby can be soothing. Does a particular kind of flower bring happy memories? Then keep a fresh bouquet of that flower around for the elder. Ask family members to share a bouquet each week during the winter instead of remembering Valentine's Day with six or seven bouquets.

Keeping photographs of people and places important in the life of the elder nearby can be not only comforting but a good way to make conversation and connection. Putting labels in the corner of picture frames—whether they are by the bed or on the wall—allows elders a way to remember. Often it is easier for elders to tell stories of long ago than to recall what happened yesterday or an hour ago.

CARING FOR PETS

If the elder's household has an animal companion, make sure the pet's needs are assessed and met. Showing you care about what is important to the elder creates good feelings. You will be in charge of all aspects of that pet's care—feeding, cleaning, brushing, playing, exercising, vet care; however, the elder may derive great satisfaction from helping with that care, and the animal may instinctually know how to elicit that attention from the elder. Is the elder still able to go for walks with a dog? Great! Perhaps the elder is able to walk but not control the leash. Maybe the animal likes to play, but the elder is too frail to do that anymore. You play with the cat or dog while they watch. Have fun!

NURTURING PLANTS

If the elder has plants, keeping them healthy will help your elder stay healthy and happy. Plants add oxygen to the environment, plus they give you something to talk about, "Oh, look, the hibiscus is going to have another bloom." During the summer it is cheery to see colorful flowers in pots or planters just outside the window or door.

INVOLVING THE ELDER

From some elders you may learn a different lesson. A desire to be "of use" is fundamental to their well being.

For some who always liked to cook, clean, and do household chores, letting them help or instruct you might be good for them. Although the elder might tire easily, it feels good to help. Keep elders involved in what is important to them. Maybe vacuuming is too much of an effort, but dusting is good. Perhaps washing the dishes by hand feels good to old arthritic fingers. Allow elders to participate in normal activities as long as possible. Watch and be ready to assist them with a follow-up chair, drink of water, and an energy-producing snack.

ORGANIZING THE KITCHEN

Keeping the kitchen in shape is a system in which all will participate. Prepared foods in the refrigerator and extra portions stored in the freezer, all in appropriate containers, need to be labeled and dated. You might find cans and boxes stashed away in cupboards, pantries, or food storage rooms that are older than the hills. Inventory everything to make sure there is nothing unsafe. Discard what is questionable. A well-stocked household allows caregivers choices in what to serve to the elder and themselves. Make sure there is a perpetual shopping list posted for whomever does the shopping. A whiteboard with dry markers in the kitchen is helpful for lists that change. Or it may be as simple as a small note-pad taped to a cupboard or the refrigerator.

Caregivers who like to cook can easily make larger portions of stews, soups, and entrées stored for later. Fresh fruit cut into bite-size pieces is easy for elders to eat any time they have low energy. Most elders seem to crave sweets. Consider keeping some good-quality dark choco-late around. Offer a bowl of ice cream. There are candies that are made without sugar for those who are diabetic. It's not about doing without, but it concerns finding the things that bring comfort. There are additional sugges-tions in the chapter about food and nutrition.

ADDING OTHER CAREGIVERS

To keep a household running, it is essential to find good caregivers. Your doctor's office might have sug-gestions. Networking through friends is helpful. The local hospital, the office of the aging, and senior centers generally keep lists. References and recommendations are vital. Interviewing each candidate is important. Ask for resumes and the scope of work the potential employee is used to doing. Although having a Certified Nursing Assistant degree is helpful, you may decide that it is not a necessary qualification for every caregiver. It takes a team to care for elders, and each brings valuable skills.

The elder also has a say. There are some personalities that just don't mix well. Each caregiver needs to have an introductory period of time with the elder—a friendly conversation before hiring. If the elder dislikes someone, then it would be counterproductive to have that person in the household. It could lead to real agitation for your elder instead of companionship and security. Create an environment in which you and the elder are comfortable.

Consider your elder as you contemplate hiring other caregivers. The person hired might be called upon to lift your elder at some time, so stamina and good physical health are integral. The elder might be more comfortable with male or female caregivers, perhaps those of a particular age group. Variety brings stimulation.

Moving the Household

It is too often true that an elder must move from the home in which they have lived for a long time. It's important to frame that reality in a way to least traumatize your elder. Being able to see the new place is important. Careful planning of the furniture and possessions that will travel with the elder and how those things will fit in the new home is a big decision that deserves careful consideration. Making floor plans to organize the new space is a helpful step. Be sure that treasured items that don't fit are passed to the people your elder wishes to have them.

It will take much time and effort to accomplish the results of a smooth transition. It is worth it. Knowing the importance to the elder makes it worthwhile.

It isn't always easy to know who will provide the perfect home for pets that cannot be accommodated in the new living arrangement. Network the information through all of the relatives and friends, the senior center, and the local animal adoption center. Make posters with the animal's pictures and a brief explanation. Start early. And don't forget the local veterinarian offices as networking sites. Consider calling an animal whisperer or pet psychic, knowing that the happiness of the elder and the animal are both in the balance.

If plants cannot accompany your elder, brainstorm about who you know is interested in plants and who has room for them. Go through the lists of people and places. Maybe a favorite dentist or doctor has room in the office.

There are businesses that specialize in moving elders. They take on responsibilities from packing and moving, to organizing garage sales and donating leftover articles to charity, to cleaning the vacant house. They put part of the proceeds of the sale against their bill and the rest goes to the elder.

CONCLUSION

The purpose of the whole assembled team is the comfort of the elder. Everyone working together can provide a smoothly run household that allows the elder a sense of security and well-being.

❧

". . . I KEEP PICTURING ALL THESE
LITTLE KIDS IN THIS BIG FIELD OF RYE
AND ALL. THOUSANDS OF LITTLE KIDS,
AND NOBODY'S AROUND—NOBODY BIG, I
MEAN—EXCEPT ME. AND I'M STANDING ON
THE EDGE OF SOME CRAZY CLIFF. WHAT I
HAVE TO DO, I HAVE TO CATCH EVERYBODY
IF THEY START TO GO OVER THE CLIFF—I
MEAN IF THEY'RE RUNNING AND THEY
DON'T LOOK WHERE THEY ARE GOING I
HAVE TO COME OUT FROM SOMEWHERE
AND *CATCH* THEM. THAT'S WHAT I DO ALL
DAY. I'D JUST BE THE CATCHER IN THE RYE
AND ALL. I KNOW IT'S CRAZY, BUT THAT'S
THE ONLY THING I'D REALLY LIKE TO BE."

~ J. D. SALINGER,
FROM HIS BOOK
Catcher in the Rye

~ 3 ~

Learning that Safety Is No Accident

~~~~~~

S afety trumps everything else in importance. That's it. On every level, safety is the bottom line. A client was once quite insistent that he did not need a caregiver in the house, although he was old and frail, and the family and doctor both insisted upon the presence of a caregiver. He was holding fast to his refusal to cooperate with added night-time caregivers. I told him that I understood that sometime he will die, because everyone does, but I couldn't tolerate it if he hurt himself. He laughed, took it well, and agreed that hospital care, broken bones, and pain were to be avoided.

Safety has many aspects. A conscientious caregiver does everything possible to anticipate problems. Timing and attitude become really important. There are so many incremental steps on the path of elders' declining physical abilities. As a caregiver, you observe and make note of any potential hazards along each step.

Assessing Safety Measures

In most communities, home care and hospice agencies will do home assessments for safety. Sometimes it is the local hospital or the fire department. The Boy Scouts even have a checklist in their safety merit badge book that you could consult.

It's undeniable that the need for more safety features in the home accelerates with age. Here are some features to be aware of:

- Better lighting, including night lights
- Strong, sturdy full-length handrails—indoors and out—on both sides of stairs
- Uncluttered stairs, hallways, and walkways
- Nonskid mats and rugs
- Sidewalks clear of ice and snow
- Lowered water heater thermostats
- Smoke detectors
- Carbon dioxide detectors

ADAPTING BATHROOMS

Bathrooms are extremely treacherous places. There are many ways that they can be made safer. Adaptive equipment, such as handles in the tub, shower stools, and handheld nozzles can reduce the risks of falling. Height-adjustable toilet chairs without the pot are great as shower seats since the open bottom allows access for cleaning private parts. Easily installed arms for toilets are very practical. Sometimes these precautions are met with loud protestations from the elder about not needing any help: "Those things are for *old* people." It's a delicate matter. What's important is keeping the elder

"Let's just try this for a while. If you don't like it, then we can take it off later."

secure. Be soft in your approach when discussing safety. Suggesting a trial period is a good compromise: "Let's just try this for a while. If you don't like it, then we can take it off later." Sometimes the changes are accepted, and what seemed so monumental fades into just the way things are. You might even get an admission that "It sure is easier now."

MONITORING DRIVING

Whether an elder should retain a driver's license is a tricky issue. Safety should win out every time. Living with the results of an accident that harms the elder or others just isn't worth it. On the other hand, if the elder can pass a driving test done by your state's Department of Transportation, then with careful consideration, the decision can be deferred. Ride with them once in a while to see how they do. If you stay relaxed, they will be less nervous. A general rule of thumb within the medical community is that anyone with a memory loss ailment should not be driving, as any diagnosed condition will inevitably advance inhibiting cognitive function.

Losing driving privileges can feel like a huge hole in an elder's world. Be realistic. Don't lecture. Be kind. Before you talk about it, do some thoughtful research and come up with alternatives and possibilities. Offer to drive the elder in a schedule that fits yours. Have a caregiver available to do the errands with the elder. See if the stores you frequent make deliveries. See if transportation is offered by a local senior center or office for the aging. Check out the local bus system for convenient stops and timing of neighborhood routes. Elders sometimes have carpools or make trade agreements. "If you drive me to the grocery store and the pharmacy, I'll buy you lunch." See if you can help build the bridges that keep life flowing.

It is very important for elders to continue social routines, as it contributes to their wellness on every level. Perhaps you may offer a scenic drive once in a while to get your elder out of the house.

IMPLEMENTING SAFETY WHILE OUTSIDE THE HOME

Sometimes it is the lack of paying attention to little details that may cause suffering. Before any dental visit, especially when anesthesia is involved, elders need to be well fed. Waiting for normal sensations in the mouth to return takes too long, and elders tend to bite their tongues and cause injury if they need to eat too soon. Thinking ahead about the elder's comfort is always important. Any appointment can take too long. Make sure your elder is fed and makes a bathroom visit before going anywhere. Take some small snacks and a water bottle along in your bag. Elders don't have enough stamina to wait when they are hungry or thirsty, and they often cannot tell when they are becoming dehydrated.

When walking, always take an arm or hand and watch for and warn about potential hazards such as stairs, slopes, and icy walkways.

USING PERSONAL ALARM DEVICES

These are invaluable. The devices are worn as bracelets or necklaces. In case of an emergency, all one needs to do is push the button and help will arrive. The monthly fee is small compared to the elder's sense of security.

Make sure that smoke and carbon monoxide detectors are inside the home and in working condition.

ASSISTING WITH MOBILITY

As an elder's mobility diminishes, stay ahead of the curve. Chivalry is not dead. Always have a firm hold on an elder when walking in uncertain terrain or have them hold onto you. Make sure the elder has the support needed, whether it is a cane or a walker or a wheelchair. Have the appropriate tools available. At every stage it is important to take the right action without waiting too long. Don't wait until an elder breaks a hip before getting walking assistance. Pay attention and listen to your intuition. Don't be fearful. Trust that you will know when to suggest further help for your elder.

Remember "Pride comes before a fall"? So often elders know they need help, but they resist utilizing aid of any kind. They don't want to appear in front of anyone using their walker. It's both silly and dangerous. Once again, here is the opportunity to be reassuring and soothing as you assist your elder with walking aids.

OBSERVING LIMITATIONS

It's helpful to check cupboards in the kitchen, bathroom,

and closets. Move things to shelves that are easy to reach. It's also important to remember that you could be a hazard. Before backing up, check to see if an elder is behind you, giving them time to move out of the way. Never push open a door if the elder could be on the opposite side of the door. Wait to hear a response before opening the door.

PREPARING FOR EMERGENCIES

Emergency preparedness is important in your home and in the home of your elder. Make sure there are needed supplies in case the power is out. Have flashlights by the bedside and other appropriate places. Have extra batteries. A battery-operated radio can let you tune in to the world. Have adequate bottled water and juices, canned and dried foods that need no preparation, and a manual can opener. Don't forget pet food. Make sure your elder has backups of needed medical supplies and eyeglasses. Consider how you will keep warm if the power is out for an extended period of time. Sleeping bags, space blankets, and hand warmers are all good to keep around.

Have a minimum of three days' water supply stored

in the event the household should need to maintain itself. Water can be stored in gallon containers with a few drops of bleach and then changed every six months. A gallon of water per day per person is the rule of thumb for water storage.

APPLYING FIRST AID

It's a good idea to take a simple course on first aid from community education or your local Red Cross. Purchase a book on basic first aid and keep it handy around the house. Get a first aid certificate, keep it up to date, and consider taking additional training, especially courses in caring for elders.

FALLS

If an elder falls, do not move her until you know she is okay. Talk to her. Ask simple questions for her to answer: "Do you know where you are?" "What day is it?" Make her comfortable. Cover her with a blanket to keep her warm until help arrives. Do not injure yourself trying to move her; however, you should know how to lift people and objects without straining your back.

STROKE

Recognize the symptoms of a stroke and get help for the sufferer as fast as possible. Ask the person to SMILE. Ask the person to TALK. Give any simple sentence and ask the person to repeat it. Ask the person to RAISE BOTH ARMS. If they have trouble doing any one of those things, then call 911. Another test is to ask him to stick out his tongue. If the tongue goes to one side or the other but not straight out, it is another indicator of a stroke. Many doctors suggest giving an aspirin to someone who might have had a stroke. It is as a good prophylactic as it acts to open the blood vessels.

Never hesitate to ask for help if needed. This is really important. Whether it regards a fall or any other circumstance, if you feel you are in over your head in any situation, ask for help. Remember, the faster a stroke victim is treated, the less damage is incurred from the stroke.

❧

~~~~~~

"MY BIGGEST SINGLE MISTAKE WAS NOT
FINDING A DOCTOR WITH EXPERTISE
IN GERIATRICS TO QUARTERBACK HER
CARE AND ATTEND TO THE QUALITY OF
HER LIFE, NOT MERELY ITS LENGTH. . . .
[THERE IS] NO WAY OF KNOWING WHAT'S
GOING TO HAPPEN NEXT SO YOU CAN
PLAN ACCORDINGLY. PHYSICIANS, SOCIAL
WORKERS, CASE MANAGERS, LAWYERS AND
FINANCIAL ADVISERS WITH EXPERTISE IN
OLD AGE ARE THE BEST GUIDES."

~ JANE GROSS, *New York Times,*
FROM HER BLOG THE NEW OLD AGE:
"WHAT I WISH I'D DONE DIFFERENTLY"

~~~~~~

~ 4 ~

Navigating Doctors, Insurance, and Finances

It is said that laughter is the best medicine. Keep a sense of humor while dealing with the difficulties of caring for a person who is close to your heart but is declining. You are the defender and protector, but don't take the difficulties too seriously or too personally. Keep a clear head, and don't let the absurdities of some situations bother you. You might even feel like laughing.

SERVING AS ADVOCATE

It is difficult to imagine what the final years of life would be like for an elder without the support and help of family and caregivers. Having a good doctor is a gift. Knowing when invasive procedures are inappropriate and when it is time for comfort care makes quite a difference in the final stages of a person's life.

Older people often give up their power to doctors. In general, they do not handle authoritarian figures with the same wisdom and clarity they displayed in their interactions before they became frail or ill. Elders need advocates to make sense of their medical care. Remember that as the advocate, you are the eyes and ears of the elder. It is your responsibility to ask the hard questions about care, to tell the doctor what changes are occurring, and to make sure the doctor understands.

VISITING THE DOCTOR

Before going to see any medical professional, it is important to have written a list of current symptoms and concerns. Write down the questions you need answered. During medical visits or when receiving consultation over the phone, write down everything the doctor or nurse says in a small notebook, whether it is an answer to a question or it is specific information. Make sure that your elder has an advocate present during all medical visits. Let the elder ask questions and give answers while you observe how the elder handles the interaction. Be prepared to speak up in cases in which the elder does not give a full or correct answer.

Some doctors are reluctant to give bad news. It is counterproductive not to tell a patient negative test results or the finding of a terminal disease. Every patient deserves honesty. Even if the diagnosis is not what you and your loved one wish to hear, knowing the truth allows both of you to plan for the future.

It is common for elders to have urinary tract infections. If an elder is prescribed an antibiotic for an infection, ask that the bacteria be cultured to see if the antibiotic is the appropriate one. Courses of antibiotics that beat down an infection for a little while—but don't kill it—destroy the beneficial flora of bacteria in the body. This can lead to a general weakness and any number of other health crises. Probiotics and cranberry juice, especially undiluted and unsweetened, or cranberry tablets seem to be good preventatives for infections.

Sometimes overzealous nurses or aides set up programs or restrictions meant to be of help. If you sense that a course of action does not sound right, always check with the primary care physician. For instance, an elder who is prone to infections or dehydration may be ordered to drink six big glasses of water a day. In some cases this might make sense, but for a slight elder with a weakened heart, it could be counterproductive or even fatal to have increased activity on the heart. Some activities can cause the vital signs to spike, and resting would be more productive. During fragile times, elders may need to have their blood pressure and heart rate checked every few hours; but at other times, it may produce too much stress.

Learning about Medications

Learn what certain medications do. If a doctor changes a medication, ask, "What changes may we expect to see in behaviors, side effects, and symptoms, and for what amount of time?" Ask if medications will dehydrate the elder. Will this medication contribute to an itching or scratching behavior? Is there a best time of day to take this medication? Utilize the Internet to read about medications.

Sometimes, when an elder patient is seeing more than one medical practitioner—the general practitioner, a cardiologist, and a gynecologist, for example—the doctors will have conflicting opinions or advice. Make sure that all the medical professionals have an updated list of medications. If there is a difference of opinion between doctors about medication choices, tell the doctors about it and ask them to clarify their reasoning.

Pharmacists are a wealth of information. Ask your pharmacist about the effects of medications or the combinations of medications your elder is taking. They know when generic drugs are appropriate. They can help with your concerns about or choices of nutritional supplements.

If memory loss or dementia is a concern in the elder, do not ignore it or put off discussion or treatment. Ask the doctor for an extended visit of at least thirty minutes to have your elder complete an MMSE or other memory test. If the doctor will not make that amount of time available, seek a different doctor. Sooner is better to start on the drugs that affect neuro-receptors. The way in which those drugs work is very simple. The drugs allow the brain cells that receive and hold thoughts to stay open longer. This gives a better chance of thoughts connecting. It is very important in degenerative diseases of cognitive impairment and dementias that the elder and the family are aware of the diseases early so that they have time to plan for the future before the elder is too impaired to make decisions.

If the elder is experiencing agitation or anxiety, a bit of medication can have an amazing calming effect. It improves the quality of life to be relieved of needless worry and anxiety.

DISPENSING MEDICATION

As time goes on, the amount of medications taken by most elders increases. It is important to know if the elder is competent to handle the dispensing of those drugs. Perhaps the elder is capable of taking medications as part of a daily morning and evening routine; however, it makes sense to help with the structuring of those routines. The weekly pillbox trays with flip-top compartments make the remembering much easier for the elder. One trick is to use a clear container for day/morning and a dark colored one for evening/night medications. Label the containers with the name and time of day.

Have a written or computer-printed copy of the specific medications and nutritional supplements for each container. Tape one to the cupboard door where medications are stored and another in the purse or wallet of the elder. The sorting task only has to be done once a week. Have the same person handle it each week because then it is in one person's head when it is time to refill prescriptions. After the meds trays are filled for the week, put the bottles away to prevent misuse. Skipping medications or taking them twice can have any number of detrimental effects.

HANDLING MEDICAL INSURANCE

Handling medical insurance for an elder can be like navigating a mine field. There is no avoiding it. If an elder has come under your care, it is extremely unlikely that that particular elder is capable of taking care of this responsibility without help. It has to be done. Organize the elder's pertinent paperwork in file folders or manila envelopes. Keep them handy. Establish written legal access to your elder's financial records. Make sure that you have a signed consent form filed with the elder's primary physician and the insurance carrier, allowing you to have full access to the person's files. Always make sure that the elder is preapproved for any treatment or procedure.

Navigating discussions with an insurance company is an excellent time to do visualization. Picture it easy. Picture success. Picture that the person on the other end of the conversation wants to help you. Picture yourself gracefully navigating all of the steps needed. It takes patience, humor, and kindness on your part as well as theirs. It is helpful to know that the health insurance representative is not allowed to hang up on you. If ninety-nine out of one hundred interactions the health insurance representative fields each day are contentious, then be that one in one hundred who is patient, kind, and a good listener. Remember to take notes. Record the date, the representative's name, and the insurance carrier. Document every phone inquiry and interaction.

Formulating Advanced Directives

Advanced directives are a vital set of legal documents that set forward the elders' wishes. The Patient Self-Determination Act is a federal law to "provide written information to adult patients concerning a patient's right under state law to make decisions concerning medical care, including the right to accept or refuse medical or surgical treatment and the right to formulate advanced directives."

Life is easier if elders make decisions that provide guidelines for their families and doctors and that protect their own right to medical care. At a time when elders are relaxed and clear thinking, before any medical crisis clouds their mind and inhibits their normal activities, introduce them to the packet of advanced directives. Go through the materials slowly and patiently, piece by piece. This may include a living will, a Durable Power of Attorney for health care, a health care proxy, and a Do Not Resuscitate Order.

Explain the intent and the actuality of these documents. Give the elder time to read them and think about them. Let the elder know that it is okay to ask questions. If you don't know the answers to the questions they have, assist in finding out. Talk it over with family members. Urge your elder or help your elder talk with her doctor, attorney, or minister if she so chooses.

Addressing Financial Concerns

Seek the help of a financial counselor to understand how to best utilize the elder's assets to ensure proper care. It can be quite confusing to know the best path. Retaining or selling a home, taking advantage of reverse mortgages, putting properties in a son or daughter's name—all may need to be explored. If the elder's best wishes are your intention, then you are on the right track.

Sometimes it becomes evident that the elder needs a different standard of care than you are able to give. A family might have been doing their best to care for an elder at home, but there might come a time when a nursing home is the right choice for the intense needs. Patients afflicted with dementia who no longer recognize loved ones or familiar surroundings may become unruly and abusive. It is important to recognize the appropriate time for appropriate action. There is no reason for guilt. It becomes the time for making the best decision you can.

Some geriatric social workers recommend that family members and caregivers give their elders reassurance that they will always be there for them, but making promises to your elder such as "You will never have to leave your home" is inappropriate.

One woman discovered that the most economical end of her life was to donate her body to science. She made prior arrangements that, after her death, her body would be transported to the hospital by ambulance at no cost. Her remains would be cremated at no cost. The only expense incurred would be the postage on her ashes being mailed to her daughter. The choice may seem absurd to some, but the choice was hers to make. Her wish was to avoid being a financial burden.

❦

~~~~~~

"THE IMPORTANT PART OF FISHING
AIN'T THE FISH, BUT THE FISHING.

THE IMPORTANT PART OF LOVING
IS TO LOVE.

THE IMPORTANT PART OF DOING
MOST ANYTHING YOU'RE DOING

IS DOING IT WITH ALL OF YOUR HEART.

'CUZ IF THE FISH DON'T BITE,
YOU'VE STILL GOT THE WATER

AND THE TREES AND THE SKY UP ABOVE."
~ TIM BAYS,
"THE IMPORTANT PART OF FISHING,"
FROM THE BEN WINSHIP ALBUM *Fishing Music*

~~~~~~

~5~

Devising Activities for Fun and Stimulation

Just because people get older does not mean they are ready to stop having fun. Keeping active is important. Seniors who engage in all kinds of activities keep their vitality. Look for things you can enjoy doing together. Focus on the enjoying. Relish the moments of pleasure. Seek out the circles of people who can engage in shared activities your elder enjoys. Do what you can to facilitate the logistics of those activities.

When your elder is in social situations, it is important that they feel comfortable. It's embarrassing and distressing for the elder and others not to remember people or their names. Take it upon yourself to help them feel at ease. When someone approaches, say, "Oh, look. Here comes Sally Brennan. She was in your old book club." If you don't know the person who comes over to speak to the elder, then introduce yourself and say, "I'm sorry, but I've forgotten your name. I'm Geraldine." That allows both your elder and the other person to avoid feeling awkward.

DISCOVERING INTERESTS

What can you do to keep up with the ongoing and add to the new? So much might be slipping away from your elder that it is important that you find things to do together on a regular basis. Keeping active in mind and body is what it is all about. The quietest of all activities is listening. Engage in conversations about what the elder likes or liked to do. Elders might be reluctant to speak, as they might be slower in gathering and formulating thoughts, but it is essential for creating trust and good-will. If you are patient, listening might reveal some of the activities the elder cherishes.

Look around the house for evidence of your elder's lifelong activities. The types of books your elder collects may be an indication of interests in gardening, cooking, birding, architecture, art, poetry, historical fiction, or

A woman in her nineties is still inspired to keep up with her life list of birds. She and her son drive to varied terrains, walk along pathways, or sit by a body of water and exchange viewing tips and conversation with other birding enthusiasts. Sometimes she needs help getting her eye on the birds, but she gets out and tries. When the tiny warblers are migrating in the spring and her favorites come back on schedule, she's right there with her binoculars around her neck. Keeping track of her day lists, year lists, and life list helps to keep her mind sharp. Being out in nature on a spring morning is also an inspiring way to start the day.

This same woman had always been a good baker, keeping her family supplied with wonderful pies, cakes, cookies, and shortcake biscuits. Her other son now bakes with her—finding and reading recipes, measuring and mixing, timing the baking—keeping her alert and active. Everyone still enjoys the results of her labor.

mysteries. Maybe your elder belonged to a book club. What do the photo albums tell you? Did your elder tango, sing, perform, fish, or travel? A musical instrument, a stamp collection, even decks of cards may indicate a passion or an amusing diversion that was once important to the elder. Talking about those activities with the elder does not have to be the end. Maybe you will discover interests you have in common, making it easier to enjoy time together.

Whether it is square dancing or solving crossword puzzles, walking or playing computer games, being active helps to keep the brain stimulated. Staying involved with

A 98-year-old man's favorite time of every week is when his caregiver takes him out to the local diner for a burger and a beer. They visit with the regular customers. They play a few favorite tunes on the jukebox and sing along. They have a nice drive, and the caregiver describes the scenery since the man's eyesight is quite diminished. They have fun.

contemporaries keeps a balance in an elder's life. What activities does your community have to offer seniors?

Offering Physical Activities

Look for new ways to exercise the elder's body as a chance to build brain power. Activities that program the body to move in new ways stimulate both mind and body. Perhaps the local YMCA or recreation center offers water aerobics, yoga, Tai Chi, or line dancing. Often health insurance plans cover some classes that help maintain fitness. Gardening is a wonderful pastime. Modern practices like French intensive gardening in raised beds allow even those in wheelchairs to get their hands in the soil and experience the pleasure of watching plants grow. The rewards of looking at beautiful flowers and eating vegetables raised by one's own skills are many.

Taking a daily walk, as long as there are no obstructions to cause a fall, is a solid form of aerobic fitness. Many facilities, including National Park Service locations, have wheelchair-accessible boardwalks and pathways, and even supply the wheelchairs.

UTILIZING MENTAL EXERCISES

Mahjong, dominos, book discussion groups, books in large print, books on tape, movie outings, jigsaw puzzles, crossword puzzles, Sudoku, bingo, bridge, canasta, pinochle, and other games all stimulate brain cells to fire. All of these things utilize memory recall. Music and art therapy are great for putting the senior in touch with feelings. Computers, cell phones, and other electronic devices can be purchased with larger knobs, buttons, and keypads for more feeble hands and larger visual displays for easy reading. Handheld games on

A circle of ladies plays Mahjong every week. They love the competition and conversation. They have lunch. They know who is up or down a dollar. Every summer they stay a few days at the historic Yellowstone Lake Hotel, enjoying the view and the chamber music played in the lounge in the afternoons while they play their game.

computer and video directed toward elders are emerging. Help your elder set up e-mail for communication with friends and family members. Scan photos for the elder to send to others.

The Educational Kinesiology Foundation has a little manual called "Brain Gyms." These simple exercises activate whole-brain learning. They take just a few minutes each day. They allow the emotions to calm, the brain to function more effectively, and equilibrium to be restored, all contributing to whole brain learning by utilizing different parts of the brain in the exercises. All these aspects are tied together by reminding people to drink more water. Water increases the electrical conductivity of the body and elevates oxygen uptake.

JOINING CHURCH-CENTERED ACTIVITIES

Church may be the center of an elder's spiritual practice. Staying in touch with one's beliefs can be a powerful force for good as one faces the large philosophical questions of the universe. Church groups have all kinds of activities that might benefit your elder. Volunteering in the community may be something that has been part of your elder's life, and churches are a good avenue for those activities. It may be important to your elder to remain part of the sewing circle or to help with the food bank. These are wonderful opportunities to socialize and feel useful.

Reading Poetry

There is something about the rhythm of poetry that is quite appealing to the ear. You might find a volume of old poems in the elder's household, or you can certainly pick one up from the local library. Poems that coincide with seasons or holidays can help the elder remember the time of year. Some elders love to hear poems read again and again. Most elders went to school at a time when they had to memorize poetry in school, and you might be surprised that someone who can't remember your name can still recite several long poems.

"Big bugs have little bugs on their backs to bite 'em. And little bugs have lesser bugs and so on, ad infinitum."

—*Anonymous,*
parodying Jonathan Swift's
On Poetry: A Rhapsody

One man repeated this rhyme that he had learned from his botany professor seventy years before. He recalled the name of the professor, and he laughed each time he said the rhyme.

RECORDING FAMILY HISTORY

Another activity is to either act as scribe while the elder tells stories from his or her life, or hire a professional to help the elder get a family or personal history down in writing. Generations of future family members might be forever grateful. Some elders get a lot of satisfaction doing genealogical research. You may find invaluable help in these projects from your local historical society. They often have oral history initiatives that include lines of questions that stimulate memory recall and recorders to loan for that purpose.

It is not the activity itself but the enrichment of the day for both caregiver and elder that is the reward.

One elder in an advanced stage of dementia would sometimes experience agitation and begin a relentless chant of, "I want to go home." The dedicated team of caregivers came up with an innovative solution. They took him to his room and helped him pack a bag. They then took him for a drive in a car. After a diversion, they turned around and headed back. The man would ask, "Where are we going?" With great reassurance, they told him, "We are taking you home!" And they did. The effect lasted a couple of weeks, and then they would take him home again.

~~~~~~

"LADIES BATHED BEFORE NOON, AFTER
THEIR THREE O'CLOCK NAPS, AND
BY NIGHTFALL THEY WERE LIKE SOFT
TEACAKES WITH FROSTINGS OF SWEAT AND
SWEET TALCUM."

~ HARPER LEE,
FROM HER BOOK
To Kill a Mockingbird

~~~~~~

~6~

Implementing Personal Care

~~~~~~

T here are many reasons why elders tend to overlook the importance of hygiene and personal care as they age: It's too much trouble. They are afraid of falling or getting too cold. They fear they might not be able to get out of the tub. Their sense of smell has diminished so they don't realize they might have body odor or bad breath. They are too tired. They can't remember when they last showered and it seems like yesterday. They are unable to see the stains on their clothes. They aren't going anywhere, so who will know the difference? Hot water costs too much.

It helps to consider personal care from the elder's point of view. Through understanding, it might be easier to figure out a routine to help the elder with personal care. It is important to be honest. If someone has bad breath or body odor, it's better to tell them in a gentle manner than to wish you could avoid being near. The elder's intention is not to offend. Telling the truth gently is a genuine way of caring and adds the bond of integrity to your relationship. You wish the best for your elder.

CREATING PERSONAL ROUTINES

Daily routine is important for your elder. Starting fresh at the beginning of the day means some preparation is done at night after the elder goes to bed. Take all clothes worn that day straight to the laundry after they are removed. Lay out clean clothes. Place the toothbrush, toothpaste, hairbrush, and a clean washcloth by the bathroom sink in the same place for each morning's activities. In the morning, with all kindness, remind your elder of the steps to be taken and then talk about what's for breakfast after the morning toilette is accomplished. Unless your elder is seriously ill, he should be encouraged to get dressed every day.

Maybe it's more in line with the elder's schedule that

he comes to the breakfast table in a robe and, after some nourishment, proceeds with the dressing and cleaning. The point is to make it a daily ritual that brings comfort in its familiarity. Give encouraging compliments: "My, do you smell good!" "That's a great shirt. It brings out the color of your eyes." If he needs help picking an outfit, it might be nice to remind him who gave him the shirt he is contemplating wearing that day. Your elder may need help with dental care such as floss holders or a soft toothbrush with an adaptive handle. Ask the dentist or doctor for new innovations in technology to make these tasks easier.

BATHING

Honor your elder's wishes in their choice of bath or shower. Adaptive equipment such as shower chairs and handheld nozzles help them feel secure and comfortable.

Maybe evening is what fits best in the elder's life for a bath or shower. It might be a relaxing routine before changing into night clothes and watching a favorite TV show. However, some elders can be very clever about avoiding baths. They can be quite convincing about saying they took a bath last night after you left. Bargaining is a good option. Tell your elder that if she takes a bath, you'll read her another chapter of the book you are reading or give a back or foot rub. Arranging the towels in a certain way before you leave is a clever way of checking if a bath actually happened.

Often modesty plays a part in the aversion to bathing. Drawing a bath or preparing everything for a shower, then staying close by but out of the bathroom, can work as long as the elder does not need assistance. As time goes by, your elder will need more help. If you are gentle and modest, but not embarrassed, you will help the elder to feel okay about it, too. We all live in bodies. It's okay.

HAND WASHING AND SKIN CARE

Reminding your elder to wash her hands is vital to keep the elder free of infections. One of the common aspects of dementia is obsessively scratching the skin of the face or arms or legs. Those gouges in delicate skin can become quite acute. Clean hands help reduce infections. Keeping fingernails cut short helps, too.

Antibiotic salves and lotions can sometimes reduce the urge to scratch and promote healing. Most elders love to have the lotions and salves applied to their skin by a caregiver. Don't be afraid to touch your elder. Rubbing in lotion or massaging in a salve brings a great deal of comfort as well as the needed medication. Just be careful if they are ticklish.

Antibiotic wipes are extremely useful for all kinds of accidents. Keep some on the bathroom counter. Some caregivers utilize latex gloves. It's important to be conscientious about washing your own hands often to prevent spreading germs to your elder. Medical professionals say that a fifteen-second regimen of rubbing your hands with soap is a minimum.

FOOT CARE

One of the hardest aspects for elders seems to be caring for their feet. Feet tend to become a source of health problems. Feet are hard to reach. Toenails tend to get thick and hard. Those aged feet have carried their person for a long time. Did the elder wear high heels for too many decades? Did they have their feet jammed into pointy-toed cowboy boots? As is the habit of most elders, do they put on yesterday's socks and shoes the minute they get up and take them off when it's time for bed? Some elders' feet don't even know how to wiggle anymore. Make sure a clean pair of socks is set out for your elder along with a clean set of clothes.

In many communities there is a monthly foot clinic for seniors to attend. Some health insurance plans allow coverage for occasional visits to a podiatrist. For some ladies, a pedicure might have been part of a regularly scheduled regime that got abandoned as she aged. Schedule someone to care for your elder's feet on a monthly basis. Your local spa or hair stylist can help you locate a pedicurist.

If you are the one to care for your elder's feet, it's pretty easy. It gets easier every time you repeat the routine as the feet get in better shape and you become more assured. Supplies include several old towels, gentle soap, bath oil, strong clippers, an emery board, small scissors, and some moisturizer. Some caregivers wear latex gloves.

Make sure the elder is in a comfortable position and won't need to make haste to the bathroom once you've begun. Half fill a basin with quite warm water and a bit of gentle soap and bath oil. Place a thick towel on the floor or carpet to protect it from splashing. Roll up your elder's pant legs and gently place those old tootsies in the water. Let them soak for at least ten minutes.

Remove one foot from the water and dry it while holding it on your lap. Be gentle. Think incrementally. Don't make bold moves. Cutting or tearing the skin could lead to infections. After the nails are cut and filed, use moisturizer to soften the skin. Massage the feet to aid in circulation. Some women like to have their toenails painted after a relaxing pedicure.

After both feet are done, do a little movement therapy. Do the motions with your own feet at the same time, both to share and demonstrate for the elder. Wiggle the toes. Bend the ankles up and down, then in circles both ways a few times. Wiggle the toes again to get a bit of circulation going. Put on clean socks and leave the feet elevated on a footstool for awhile. Put shoes on your elder before helping them up to walk. Socks make it too easy to slip and fall.

HAIR CARE

For both men and women elders, it needs to be part of the routine to focus on hair care. It's important to have regular salon visits for most women. Whether it's cutting, coloring, a permanent, or just a weekly shampoo and set, it feels great. It's fun to take a man to the barbershop for a haircut and listen to the local banter. Don't forget the trimming of eyebrows as well as nose and ear hair. In the home, keep the brushes clear of hair and wash them regularly.

❧

"COOKING DONE WITH CARE IS AN
ACT OF LOVE."

~ CRAIG CLAIBORNE,
FROM HIS BOOK
Kitchen Primer

~ 7 ~

Concentrating on Food, Eating, and Nutrition

There are many things to consider when cooking for an elder person. Preparing food and eating, to elders, may seem like too much effort. They might have lost their appetite before someone started cooking for them, and they are just not used to eating anymore. Their sense of taste may have diminished or changed due to medications. Loss of appetite may be tied to depression or fear of their end of life. Maybe they just don't like to eat alone. You may also notice that if an elderly person is asked if he is hungry, he looks at his watch to see what time it is. In many instances, elders have lost touch with body sensation.

GETTING YOUR ELDER TO EAT

In some ways, providing nourishment to an elder is just like feeding anyone else. It's easier to eat if the food is good. Foods that are fresh, well prepared, in season, colorful, and tasty are more enjoyable. It's about the joy of foods and eating and the setting. Both bad food and the language you use can be extremely off-putting. How many of us remember from childhood, "You must clean your plate," "Eat your vegetables!" or "You should eat something." It didn't work then, and there is no reason to believe those tactics would work now, so don't be strident

"Here, I've made this for you
(or for us to share). See if you like it."

or demanding. Use words that entice your elder to nourish herself. Remember that most people resent being *told* what to do.

It's awfully easy to resent the word "should." There is just something about it that seems condescending. Offer invitations instead of making demands: "Here, I've made this for you (or for us to share). See if you like it."

Like many things in life, getting your elder to eat might need to start first with conversation. An element of surprise can make life interesting, but sometimes it is the familiar that reaches people. Sit down and talk about food and beverage likes and dislikes. Be specific. Share some of your own preferences as a way to get your elder to open up. Take notes. Make lists of food to avoid. Try to find out some of the favorite childhood memories that involved food. Maybe it was something that his mother or grandmother cooked well, or a place her father took her to eat. Somewhere in the elder's kitchen, you might find cookbooks and recipe boxes. Going through them might bring forth a treasure trove of favorite treats. Try the recipes that look like they have been used the most. Make it all an adventure. Make it fun.

ENJOYING THE KITCHEN

Many elders may at first be resistant to someone new taking on projects in their kitchens. They might worry about you making a mess. It is important to make yourself acquainted with the whole kitchen. Look in the cupboards and remember where things are kept. Always put things away where they belong. Be organized. Clean up as you go along in any project. When you are through, make sure the kitchen is cleaner than when you started.

Many elderly households become reduced to using paper plates and napkins when the cupboards are filled with lovely dishes, glasses, and linens. Use the finery. Create beauty. Feed all of the senses. Put flowers on the table or a sweet little plant. Present elders with some of the style they used to enjoy.

SOCIALIZING

Your elder might miss the socializing that is part of enjoying the pleasure of shared meals. Take note of the people important in your elder's life. Why not invite company to the elder's home for a meal? Don't make it too fancy or it could be stressful. One or two guests allow for comfortable conversation. Perhaps it is a favorite relative to invite. Don't forget to include the elder in the planning process. You don't want to overwhelm her, but you want her to feel a part of the fun.

One elderly woman used to love to go out to lunch with her friends. Her loss of hearing and her frailty then made that arrangement uncomfortable and inconvenient. Her caregiver suggested that she invite her friends for lunch, which the caregiver fixed and served to all. In the quiet of the woman's home, it was possible to converse and find joy in talking over old times. It was a source of happiness and stimulation for all of them to be together again.

SELECTING FAVORITE FOODS

There is such a profusion of choices in our markets these days; for some elders, there are too many choices. Most of our elders had a smaller scope in their diets. They ate what was local. They ate what was in season. Keep these things in mind when shopping and meal planning. Whether the elder you care for is from Alabama or Italy, find out what they long for and figure out how to make something almost as satisfying.

A simple fruit salad is a treat any time of year. In the summer, that can mean fresh melons and berries. Autumn is for apples, sliced on a plate or in salads or baked. Homemade applesauce is so easy to make and fills the house with an aroma that stimulates the appetite. It goes great with many meals. Winter salads might include grated carrots with raisins and pineapple or the classic Waldorf salad with diced apples, chopped celery, and toasted walnuts. One woman remembered her favorite springtime dish was new potatoes and peas from the garden, cooked in cream sauce.

Some elders have a hankering for dandelion greens in the springtime, often the first growing things they had seen in months during their childhood days. Dandelion greens are delicious if picked when they are small, before they grow bitter. There is no shortage of dandelions in this world, but make sure they haven't been sprayed. It is so easy to wash them, steam them, and serve with a little butter and a splash of apple cider vinegar.

One caregiver told me that her client would not eat sandwiches for lunch. It is easier to satisfy someone if you ask specific questions. This is what you might say: "If I were to fix you a sandwich, would you like it plain, toasted, or grilled?" And then you could continue on. Do you prefer white, wheat, or rye bread? Open faced or two slices of bread? Would you like cheese, ham, turkey, tuna, egg salad, bacon, lettuce and tomato, sliced

"If I were to fix you a sandwich, would you like it plain, toasted, or grilled?"

vegetables, avocado and tomato, grilled chicken, or fried egg? Do you like butter, mayonnaise, mustard, salsa, or cranberry sauce? Butter on one side and something else on the other? Do you like lettuce? Is it easier to handle if the lettuce is finely shredded? Do you want carrot sticks, some olives, or a pickle? What kind?

To entice someone to eat, it is okay to go outside the

boundaries. Perhaps this person only likes breakfast. Great! You have lots of choices: waffles, pancakes, crêpes, omelets, French toast, hard-boiled eggs, poached eggs, fried eggs, strata, burritos, blintzes, or muffins. Offer and serve any kind of breakfast or lunch or dinner the person wants any time of day. One client shared that she loved going to her grandmother's house when she was little. "She made the best sourdough pancakes just for me! I would eat so many." The light went on. It was easy to dig up a sourdough starter and make her pancakes for breakfast. Sure enough, she ate lots. It's easy to add bananas, blueberries, and whole-grain flours.

It's important to consider the quality of life as much as whether something is good for someone. If an elder wants bacon or sausage every day, maybe it's more important to have that person happy than to keep them alive longer facing platefuls of foods they don't like.

PLANNING NUTRITIOUS MEALS

It's perfectly okay to be both accommodating and tricky at the same time. In an attempt to get nourishment to an elder with no real desire to eat, you might turn to milkshakes. Maybe the person loves chocolate. By making a milkshake in the blender, you can utilize a whole banana, some protein powder, whole milk, ice cream, and some chocolate syrup. The elder will drink some nourishment instead of going without a meal. The same can be said for banana splits with various fruits, nuts, and maybe homemade blueberry syrup for antioxidant value and great flavor. How many things can you think of that will go in a smoothie? Be creative.

There is a whole realm of comfort foods that are nutritious and easily digested. It is really easy to bake custard, and it is especially pleasing when served in an individual cup. Old-fashioned tapioca pudding is a real treat for some elders. For our elders, there is probably a historic attachment to Jell-O. Old family favorites still whet the appetites of many Americans.

The aromas of cooking and baking wafting through the house induce appetite and the feeling of well-being. There is nothing better than the smell of homemade chicken soup. Actually, any kind of soup works well. Soup is full of good nutrient value, is easy to eat, and tastes so much better when made at home rather than emptied from a can. If you read the labels of commercially produced food, it will really encourage you to make your own soup. Elders don't need the amount of sodium that is in most store-bought brands.

Baking is wonderful therapy for the baker, the elder, and any visitors. If a caregiver must be present for hours and days, why not bake? A cookie jar filled with oatmeal cookies chockful of raisins and nuts is a welcome treat for anyone. You might bake bread weekly for the household where you give care. It might be something for your elder to share with other homebound friends. Rolls warm from the oven are great with your homemade soup. Homemade jam and toast make for a delightful breakfast.

Reading labels moved me to start making jams and jellies from the abundance of summer fruits. Store-bought jams, and many other foods, list corn syrup as their primary ingredient. It seems that fruit should top the list. Making a few batches of jam in the summer adds to the pleasure of eating all year long, especially on cold winter days. Elders who have lived in their own home a long time might have fruit trees or bushes from which to harvest berries or fruit to make preserves, jellies, or jams. Watching that fruit go to waste can be a source of stress to some elders. Do two things at once: make homemade preserves for your elder and eliminate the waste and stress.

It's easy to get elders to eat fresh ripe fruits in season. Dishes of peaches or strawberries, either plain or on their favorite cereal, are favorites with most elders.

Helpful Serving Tips

- To preserve the elder's dignity, present food in smaller pieces rather than cut it up on a plate in front of them or others.
- Utilize contrasting food colors so they show up better.
- Use soup plates instead of flat plates to help elders capture foods.
- Serve smaller portions on smaller plates for those with smaller appetites.
- Use smaller glasses. They are easier to grasp.

INTEGRATING OTHER SUGGESTIONS

Sometimes tiny meals throughout the day work better than whole meals three times a day. If the elder in your care is not eating well, try a lot of different strategies. Most of the time, elders need to take in calories. Do whatever works. Breakfasts are a good start. How many ways can you make oatmeal interesting? What can you add to give it a little zest?

For elders who must reduce their salt intake, don't salt food while you are preparing it. Let folks salt their food if they think they need to. Use reduced sodium salt in the table shaker. Use sea salt, as it has a higher, more complete mineral content and less sodium than table salt. Use herbs and spices to enhance flavors instead of salt.

Read ingredients on prepared food packaging. You will find that making food with fresh ingredients for your elder will not only be less expensive, but it will also be more flavorful and more nutritious.

Many seniors really like Turner Classic Movies, especially if the film features a favorite movie star of yesteryear or if it is a film they have seen before. Making a tray or setting a place before the television is sometimes a treat. However, if you find your elder gets too absorbed in the film and forgets to eat, retreat back to the kitchen table.

CASUAL RECIPES

"APPROACH LOVE AND COOKING WITH
RECKLESS ABANDON."
~ TENYIN GYATSO
HIS HOLINESS, THE 14TH DALAI LAMA

Cooking can be tons of fun. It's not just a chore. It's rewarding to nourish others and yourself. It's a dance. It's a meditation. It's for enjoyment. Lots of people think they don't know how to cook, that it's a mystery beyond their comprehension. Perhaps if recipes are formatted in a way to seem less serious, it might seem easier. These recipes are written conversationally, giving options to suit your tastes and creativity. Just don't take it all too seriously.

Here are some things I've found helpful:

- Before you start, read the whole recipe from beginning to end.
- Make sure you have everything you need.
- Prior to beginning to cook, lay out all of the ingredients, dishes, and utensils you will need.
- Clean up as you go along; then there is no big mess to clean up at the end. It makes the whole process seem easier.
- Make notes on the recipe pages to remind yourself of anything you discovered while making the recipe.
- When using herbs and spices, pour from the container into the palm of your hand and then into the pot or bowl. This will help in getting the amount needed.
- Select a measuring spoon, fill it with salt or sugar, level it, and then pour it into the palm of your hand. Repeat process with other spoon sizes to get a reference as to what different measurements look like.

BAKED CUSTARD

Custard may be baked in individual serving cups or in one dish. Its soothing texture makes it easy to eat as a dessert or for breakfast with fruit and maple syrup. A richer custard is achieved using part half & half instead of milk. Richer would be good for someone reluctant to eat or who needs calories. The top may be sprinkled with the traditional nutmeg before baking; brown sugar, cinnamon, or chocolate may also be used. If this recipe appeals, then perhaps old-fashioned tapioca or rice pudding will also become favorites. The preparation of both is similar to custard.

Custard is baked in a water bath. To bake, place the custard dishes in a large ovenproof baking dish, such as a sheet cake pan, that you will fill with an inch of water.

YIELDS ABOUT 6 (6-OUNCE) CUSTARD CUPS

2 eggs
4 egg yolks
⅔ cup sugar
Pinch of salt
3 cups milk, or a combination of milk and half & half
1 teaspoon vanilla extract
Sprinkle of nutmeg

~~~~~~

Preheat oven to 300 degrees F.

Whisk the eggs and egg yolks together in a medium-size mixing bowl. Add the sugar and salt. Whisk until dissolved. Gradually add the milk and stir until blended. Stir in the vanilla. Pour into custard cups or an appropriate-size glass baking dish. Sprinkle the tops with nutmeg. Set the custard dish(es) in the water bath. Place carefully in the oven. Bake until the custard seems set when carefully jiggled, about 30 to 40 minutes. (Individual cups take less time than one larger dish.) Remove from oven, taking care to not spill the hot water. Allow to cool or offer one to your elder while still warm.

After they have cooled, cover with plastic wrap, date, and refrigerate.

~~~~~~

ROBERTA'S FAVORITE OATMEAL COOKIES

There is something wonderful about having a big jar of homemade cookies on the kitchen counter. It's a great way of being hospitable. Everyone who enters the kitchen wants at least one.

Baking cookies on parchment paper is a great idea. No extra grease, oil, or spray is needed. The papers can be used many times. Clean up is easier. Cookies may cool on the papers. It is such a simple trick. Slide the paper with cookies off the tray onto the counter and use the tray with a different paper for the next round of baking.

YIELDS ABOUT 5 DOZEN COOKIES

I cup vegetable oil

I cup brown sugar

I cup white sugar

3 eggs

I teaspoon vanilla extract

I teaspoon salt

2 cups rolled oats

2 teaspoons baking soda

I teaspoon cinnamon

2½ cups flour, divided

I cup raisins

I cup pecan pieces

Preheat oven to 350 degrees F.

Cream together the vegetable oil, sugars, and eggs. Add the vanilla extract and salt; stir well. Stir in the oats. Add the baking soda and cinnamon with the first cup of flour. Mix well. Add the rest of the flour and mix until all the flour is blended in. Add the raisins and pecans. You may leave out either or add chocolate chips or dried cranberries. Try different combinations.

Using a spoon or your hands, form balls about 1 inch in diameter. The cookies will double in diameter as they bake, so leave enough space between them. Bake for about 10–12 minutes, or until golden. Under-baking makes cookies that are chewy. Over-baking makes cookies that are crunchy. A bit of extra brown or dark brown sugar also helps make cookies chewier. Extra cookies can be dated, labeled, and stored in the freezer.

~~~~~~

CHICKEN SOUP

The great thing about making soup is how flexible you can be. It's soup. It doesn't care if you add one onion or two, two carrots or three, a lot of celery or a little or none at all. Add more garlic if you like. Use a pot that is large enough to make it easy to stir. One with a cover is handy. Soup is a way of using leftovers, blending flavors, experimenting. It doesn't have to be chicken soup. Try using some beef, barley, mushrooms, and kale next time.

YIELDS 6 TO 8 CUPS

Olive oil, to cover the bottom of the pot
2 or 3 carrots, diced
2 or 3 ribs of celery, diced
2 medium yellow onions, diced
3 cloves garlic, minced
Salt and pepper to taste
Herbs of your choice
1–2 bay leaves
2 cans or 1 box organic *(if you choose)* chicken broth
2 or 3 boneless chicken breasts
¾ cup cooked or uncooked rice or pasta, optional
Fresh chopped parsley, optional

Place a soup kettle on the burner at medium heat. Add the olive oil and allow to heat while you dice the vegetables. Add vegetables as you dice them and stir occasionally. It's good to start with the carrots as they take longer to cook. Add salt and pepper and whatever herbs you like, a bit of basil or oregano or thyme or sage or any combination that smells good to you. If you are not used to using herbs, start with small amounts. Their flavors grow as they simmer.

After the onions are translucent, add the broth. You may add some water if the amount of soup seems small. Add the chicken breasts whole, cover, bring to a boil, and then turn down the heat to simmer.

Add uncooked rice or noodles, or if you have either cooked and leftover in the refrigerator, use that. If there are leftover cooked vegetables, feel free to add them to the pot. Simmer for at least half an hour.

Remove the chicken and allow to cool on a cutting board. When cool enough to handle, cut or tear into bite-size pieces. Add back to the pot. Taste the soup to see if it pleases you. Add more salt and pepper if needed. Sprinkle with parsley. Serve and enjoy.

SIMPLE SALAD WITH BASIC VINAIGRETTE

Salad dressings are so full of preservatives that you might consider making your own. It's a good idea not to eat things with ingredients you can't pronounce. In fact, your elder was born before store-bought salad dressings were invented. The clean clear tastes of oil and vinegar make salads sing.

How much salad do you need? How many people are you feeding? Is it a side salad with a lot of other courses, or are you making a salad that will be an entrée for lunch? That's how you choose the size of bowl to use. If the salad is for just a couple of people, then use a soup spoon to measure. If you are feeding a medium number, then use a serving spoon. If it's for a large crowd, then start with a really big bowl and double the amounts of oil and vinegar.

Vinaigrette

1 clove garlic
1 tablespoon mustard *(your favorite)*
3 tablespoons extra virgin olive oil
   (or part toasted sesame oil, flaxseed oil, or walnut oil)
2 tablespoons vinegar
   (balsamic, red or white wine, or rice will work)
Salt and pepper to taste
Fresh or dried herbs to taste

Smash the garlic clove with the side of a knife blade to break down the cell walls and let the flavor expand. Remove the skin. Rub the inside of the salad bowl with the clove of garlic. Put mustard into the bowl. Add olive oil (or other oils). Add vinegar and then salt and pepper to taste. Whisk until blended. Adjust the seasonings until the taste pleases you. Season with a pinch of fresh or dried herbs, if you like.

Add washed greens in bite-size pieces. Remember that a large handful of greens is enough for one person. Finely sliced cabbage is a nice addition. Grated carrots are much easier to eat then big chunks. Add any other vegetables, grated or crumbled cheeses, fruits like pears or apples, a handful of toasted nuts, just not everything in the same salad. Pick two or three additions per salad to prevent the flavors being too jumbled. Vary the ingredients to complement the rest of the meal.

Salad made in this way may be kept covered in the refrigerator for hours. This is very handy to remember when preparing to serve a dinner party with so many things that need to be done at the last minute. Toss just before serving.

Some great combinations include the following:

- Olives, cucumbers, purple onion slices, and feta cheese
- Toasted pecans, sliced pears, and your favorite blue cheese
- Crumbled cooked bacon and hard-boiled eggs
- Shredded cooked chicken, sliced apples, and diced cranberries
- Grated carrots, sliced purple cabbage, and sliced bell peppers

If you use some toasted sesame oil and rice vinegar, and add a spoonful of sugar or maple syrup, then you can make an Oriental slaw by using cabbage, bean sprouts, scallions, and toasted almonds.

You can make a summer salad of marinated vegetables, including tomatoes, roasted peppers, artichoke hearts, olives, and fresh mozzarella. Add a few leaves of fresh basil, sliced ribbon thin. Serve alone or on a bed of washed greens.

~~~~~~

MILKSHAKES OR SMOOTHIES

For these recipes, all you need is a blender, a few ingredients, and a little imagination to create delicious, nutritious beverages. It's pretty basic. Just remember to put the cover on the blender before you turn it on.

FOR MILKSHAKES: Put 1 to 2 cups milk, about equal volume of ice cream and some flavoring, chocolate syrup, or fruit in the blender and blend until smooth. To enhance the nutrient content of a milkshake for someone ill or needing calories, add a ripe banana and a couple of tablespoons of protein powder to the milk and blend before adding the ice cream.

FOR SMOOTHIES: Put an 8-ounce container of your favorite flavor of yogurt, 1 to 2 cups of fresh or frozen fruit in small pieces, and some juice or sparkling water.

CONCENTRATING ON FOOD, EATING, AND NUTRITION

PANCAKES

Pancakes are another meal capable of endless variety. They can be made with milk, buttermilk, yogurt, cottage cheese, or sour cream. Some buckwheat flour or cornmeal may be substituted instead of white or unbleached flour. Sprinkle some blueberries or sliced strawberries or bananas on the pancakes in the pan as the first side is being cooked. Serve them with maple syrup and butter or yogurt and a pile of fresh fruit. The batter may be refrigerated and used another day if you add a bit more baking powder when you are ready to use the batter again.

2 cups buttermilk

3 eggs

2 tablespoons vegetable oil

2 cups flour *(may include 1 cup buckwheat flour or cornmeal)*

½ teaspoon salt

2 tablespoons sugar

2 teaspoons baking powder

1 teaspoon baking soda

Beat the wet ingredients together in a mixing bowl. Stir the dry ingredients together in a separate bowl. Add the dry to the wet ingredients and stir minimally. Over-beating will make the pancakes tough.

The pan or griddle needs to be quite hot. Test by dropping a few drops of water on it. If they sit in place, it's not hot enough. If they disappear, it's too hot. If they dance about, it's perfect. Make one test cake to see if the batter is too thick or thin. Pour the batter from a ladle or small pitcher onto the pan in small round pools, and turn the cakes after bubbles appear, about 2–3 minutes. Only turn once. The second side will cook in about half the time.

It is a great idea to have breakfast plates prepared with servings of fruit and bacon or sausage, if desired. Plate the pancakes and serve while hot.

BISCUITS

Tender biscuits warm from the oven are irresistible. They take very little time to make and are a great addition to many meals. You'll be amazed that you didn't learn sooner.

2½ cups flour
1 tablespoon sugar, optional
1 teaspoon salt
3 tablespoons baking powder
½ teaspoon baking soda
½ cup chilled butter *(or shortening, if you must)*
1¼ cups buttermilk *(if you use milk instead, leave out the baking soda)*

Preheat oven to 425 degrees F.

It's really easy to use a food processor for the first step that combines all the dry ingredients with the butter. Pulse the processor until the mixture has the texture of sand. You may use a hand pastry blender to do the first step in your mixing bowl. After you use a food processor, pour the mixture of the dry ingredients and butter into the mixing bowl.

Make a well-like indentation in the dry ingredients and add the buttermilk. Use two forks to toss the mixture until it is uniformly moist. Add a bit more buttermilk, if needed, to make it hold together. Mix as little as possible. Working the dough too much develops the gluten in flour and makes the biscuits tough.

For basic biscuits, drop the biscuit dough in 2-inch round shapes on a baking sheet lined with parchment paper. Bake until golden brown, about 12 to 15 minutes. You may make the biscuits tiny. You may pat the dough out onto a piece of waxed paper, dust the top with flour, and cut them into cookie cutter shapes. You may put all of the dough into a lightly oiled pie pan, and then cut it into wedges after it has baked to make shortcake topped with oodles of strawberries or peaches.

Additions to biscuits might include some fresh chopped herbs like oregano or sage, some cinnamon and sugar sprinkled on top before baking, or some grated sharp cheddar tossed into the dough with the forks before you blend in the buttermilk.

Biscuits are so versatile. Serve them with butter and jelly. Serve them with gravy. Serve them anytime you want.

CREAM SAUCE

A basic cream sauce is the heart of many delicious foods. The French call it béchamel. Once you become comfortable with the simple process, you will see the ease of creating variations to suit your needs.

YIELDS 1½ CUPS

3 tablespoons butter
3 tablespoons flour
1 ½ cups milk

In a heavy-bottomed pan or a medium-size cast-iron skillet, melt the butter over medium heat. The pan needs to be large enough to stir and thick enough to keep the bottom from scorching. Remove from heat and gradually add the flour, pausing to stir so it does not become lumpy. Add about 1/4 cup milk, and then stir to make sure that there are no lumps. Add the milk in portions, continually stirring to avoid lumps. Then return to medium heat and stir or whisk until boiling point is reached and the sauce thickens. Remove from heat.

Using this recipe as a base, you may add some flavorful

cheese for a sauce for vegetables or macaroni. Use it as a base for the old-fashioned favorite creamed tuna to top biscuits or toast. Add half chicken broth instead of milk, then a sprinkling of herbs and pieces of cooked chicken or turkey, and some cooked vegetables and serve as an entrée. If you desire the sauce to be a bit thinner, increase the liquid.

"COULD WE CHANGE OUR ATTITUDE,
WE SHOULD NOT ONLY SEE LIFE
DIFFERENTLY, BUT LIFE ITSELF WOULD
BECOME DIFFERENT."
~ KATHERINE MANSFIELD,
AUTHOR

~ 8 ~

Caring for the Caregiver

~~~~~~

*I*t seems that taking care of oneself would be the most simple and evident aspect of life. Why do we need to be reminded time and again? And yet, we all do. What do airlines say in the preflight safety drill? Put on your own oxygen mask first and make sure it is working before you attempt to assist others. Perhaps it is telling of our wonderful hearts that we think about others first. However, if we do not renew and refresh ourselves, it is inevitable that we will become depleted.

Taking care of the whole being is what allows one to be present for others. Humans are resilient. There is an ability to bounce back and be stronger. Often people tend to ignore their own needs. It would be far more effective to learn new skills to maintain a greater fitness for handling the demands of daily life.

Caring for the elderly or the injured is, or can be at times, stressful, isolating, overwhelming, lonely, mundane, gross, nauseating, frustrating, boring, tedious, and humbling. Those things are in contrast, of course, to all of the more positive elements of making life better for someone. Ignoring the effects of a demanding responsibility can lead to anxiety and depression and reduce the capacity for a full life.

QUIETING ONESELF

What actions can you take to improve your physical, emotional, mental, and spiritual health? There are many pieces to the solution. Each individual develops a unique template to be in touch with oneself. Take some moments of silence to decompress and allow the inner voice to speak. Do you recall the old expression "I couldn't even hear myself think"? During times of stress, it is important to make that space and time to hear yourself. There can be so much reactive internal noise that the quieting takes time and practice. Sitting quietly and running through the day's events, it becomes easier to see them from a different angle and remove the emotional charge. Gaining that perspective will allow the mind to quiet itself. Look at your own agenda to see what can be let go. When you are with the elder, be with the elder.

TAKING A BREAK FROM CAREGIVING

Doing individual work is a good first step. Only you can deal with your own internal landscape and personal growth of consciousness. Meditation helps to calm the mind and lower blood pressure. In meditation you seek nothing, just allow yourself the time to relax. Yoga does wonders for relaxation and self-esteem. The life of a caregiver may feel like a bustle of action, but it is really quite sedentary. Yoga builds flexibility and physical strength. So many of the activities that are beneficial for elders are equally good for the individuals who care for them. When undertaking these activities with the elder, you are always attending to the elder. You need to take time to decompress away from the elder you care for. Take a walk. Go to the gym. Take a dance class. Play basketball. Swim laps. Climb a mountain. Get some fresh air and sunlight. Take a class and learn something new. Draw. Paint. Journal. Go to a funny movie. Listen to some favorite music. Feel your own independence. Make some choices for yourself.

SELECTING CAREGIVER SUPPORT GROUPS

In many communities there are support groups for caregivers. Take advantage of community resources. Seek out other caregivers through your local library, counseling center, government offices dealing with health and human services, or any of the community churches. Having a peer group to share insights with helps give perspective. Having connection to others is vital for shedding light on the burdens that being a caregiver can place upon one's shoulders. It is important to share and problem solve with those on a parallel path. It may surprise you that your input is as helpful to others as theirs is to you.

Encouraging the Emotional Health of the Caregiver

A useful exercise is to look at your emotions that come up. Don't dismiss them. Really look at each. Give each a color and a shape or personality. Listen to it. Hear what it has to say. See where it sits in your body and how you feel. Thank each for what it teaches you. Then, offer it a rest. It is time to leave you.

Practice forgiveness. There are many elements that impact your complicated life. There are people who bring up patterns or emotions that are not necessarily easy. Take a look at each person or situation as you sit quietly alone or walk in nature. Examine what the person or situation has brought to you that allows you to grow. What is no longer in the present that still causes weight to your heart and mind? See if you can see any positive intention that you might have misinterpreted. Thank yourself for getting it. Allow the energy to move on. Forgive yourself by acknowledging that you are just a mortal being doing the best you are able.

Engage in luxury for yourself, not necessarily the kind

that costs a lot of money. Have a massage and feel the knots in your neck release. Draw a bath and rest your weary bones in warm water scented with relaxing herbs like lavender or rosemary. Drink some relaxing herbal tea such as chamomile or spearmint. Have a wonderful, nutritious meal that you eat slowly and thoughtfully. Breathe deeply. Do visualizations that picture the releasing of energies from your body that are not your own. Take time for yourself. Spend some time reading a good book. It takes both active and passive elements to create balance. Listen to the quiet and trust yourself to renew what is needed.

Do not ever be afraid to seek help. The value of a good counseling session is inestimable. Having a professional for a sounding board can make a huge difference. Sometimes even the clearest thinkers can get stuck going around in circles without seeing the way out of the maze.

❧

"As you climb up that mountain into the treeless region of great heights, your fellow travelers, one by one, drop back and disappear. With the remaining few—more and more forced to select your narrowing path—you go on into an increasing loneliness. Voices quaver love, complaint or courage across the ice-field or the bottomless crevasse.

"The air is perfectly pure. The light is iridescent. There is no growth, no greenness, no intimacy. The earth itself narrows into depth, to left and right, behind and before. Vast views extend themselves in giddy retrospect and—immensely far away, with the infantile horizon coming up clearly from the mist—below and vast extends the land of memory.

"There is an icy splendor in the experience, an excitement no past adventure has afforded: the land rising, above, below, to the ineffable apocalypse.

"This is old age."

~ Katharine Newlin Burt,
from her essay
"Long in the Land"

~9~

Accepting the Final Days and Carrying Out Final Wishes

Dying is part of life. It is part of a natural progression. It isn't, or doesn't have to be, frightening. It is healthy to talk about dying. When you know that someone is close to dying or thinking about dying, it is a precious gift to allow them to talk about death. It's okay for them to say anything they wish. Be there to explore the experience in words, fearlessly. It does not matter that you don't know the answers. It does not matter if it makes tears fall from your eyes. It does not matter if the other person sees you sob and blow your nose. It is perfectly alright for the person you are with to experience and show emotions. Allow yourself to be vulnerable and present. It's appropriate to touch or hold hands, even though that might never before have been a way of expression between the two of you. Anytime is a perfect time to be available for a deep, honest conversation with a loved one. Never be reluctant to share gratitude.

There is an old spiritual that speaks of "In my time of dying." An approaching death has its own timing. All else gets put aside. It is completely natural and becomes a world unto itself. Imagine it like a trip down a river. Once you step into the boat and push off into the water, there you are. You are carried by the current, floating at its speed until you reach your destination. What you have left behind no longer matters. You are in the flow for as long as it takes.

RETURNING HOME TO DIE

Making plans for the end of life makes a big difference in the end itself. Have advanced directives been put into place? Has the decision been made if the elder wishes to be at home or to be hospitalized? There is an appropriate time to quit doing invasive procedures and implement comfort care. Even if thoughtful decisions have been made, an occurrence such as a stroke could send your loved one to the hospital. Days later it may become apparent that the end is near. If the person asks to go home, then get that person home. You might be in attendance when the oncologist in a cancer clinic says that the cancer is back and surgery is necessary. Your elder might say, "I don't want to do this anymore." It takes planning. It might necessitate an ambulance ride home and a rented hospital bed and home-care nurses.

Involving Hospice

Has hospice care been introduced? Hospice care is available for the last six months of a person's life. Hospice personnel are attuned and practiced in all of the steps necessary to see a person and those involved in a person's life to finality. If hospice is involved, they are there with all of the expertise to guide and advise the family and caregivers. In addition to nursing, hospice provides medical supplies, medicines, comfort, and counseling. They take you through the process step by step. There are no surprises, except the depth of the love that permeates the surroundings.

Including Others as Days Wind Down

As a life closes, the elder may have wishes to be carried out. There may be specific people the person wants to see again. Perhaps a clergyman or spiritual counselor might be needed to bring comfort. Maybe the person dying has a request for a special meal. Even if the person hasn't eaten for weeks, they might ask for a Thanksgiving dinner. Do what you are able to bring about peace and fulfillment.

The surroundings will become of necessity a sanctuary of quiet space as the dying person's world becomes ever smaller. It becomes evident whose presence is welcome. Those who are unable to be part of the surroundings suck the level of energy down. Those who are contributors help create an aura of well-being. The necessary tasks are accomplished. There is a growing spirit of understanding.

Where would the loved one be the most comfortable? Often it seems wrong to tuck them away in a corner bedroom. Propped up in a hospital bed looking out a window at a favorite view can be perfect with ongoing life continuing around the bed. Would fresh flowers offer a soothing effect? Is a darkened environment more comfortable? For every person, the choices are individual. Does soft music or quiet reading allow the time to pass more easily? Does the purr of a beloved cat calm the person? Do ice chips soothe the throat?

Sometimes the person who is dying needs to be given permission to go. The person might need to be told that you will be fine. You may offer assurances that their wishes will be carried out. Hearing that you will be there to care for the spouse or child they are afraid to leave behind may bring an ease in letting go of life. Yes, your faithful dog will have a loving home.

It is said that when death comes, a person goes into the light. When the end of breathing seems to hover closely, it can be a service to guide the person with gentle words to see the light inside and to move into it. Gently whispered words can be reassuring.

RESPECTING THE DECEASED'S WISHES

Carrying out the wishes of the deceased is part of the transition. To have this set of decisions in place will allow the person to pass on with more ease. What are the wishes for the body and for an appropriate service?

When you have helped in the process of assisting someone in dying and that time has passed, it is astounding to step into life again. Everything seems to be rushing past, taking no notice of how you are profoundly changed. In your close circle of friends and family, you might have a wish to share some words of what you have come to know, but your friends may not know how to react to your needs. Their eyes may avert involuntarily as they shut down to you emotionally. The typical American culture is not a culture that is accepting or comfortable with death, even though it is an inevitable part of the natural process. Others' reaction to your grief is not about you. Don't take it personally. Hopefully our society will evolve to be more in touch with and more willing to integrate difficult emotions. By volunteering to be there with someone who is dying, you are part of the societal change.

If you feel that you have no safe place to discuss your feelings, seek a bereavement group. It is a powerful tool to be with those of shared experience.

❧

"BE NOT DISTURBED ABOUT THE FUTURE,
FOR IF YOU EVER COME TO IT, YOU WILL
HAVE THE SAME REASON FOR A GUIDE
THAT YOU HAVE AT PRESENT."
~ MARCUS AURELIUS
FROM THE BOOK
The Meditations of Marcus Aurelius Antonius

~10~

Contemplating the Future of Caregiving

What will the future of elder caring look like? It is yet to be formulated. At the end of the nineteenth century, the greatest minds of the day were brought together in New York City to look at the looming catastrophe for the metropolis. At that current rate of growth, it was estimated that the streets would be knee-deep in horse manure within the next twenty years. Some things can be anticipated and others cannot.

Generations of families used to live together. The grandparents, the aged ones, cared for the infants while the grown-ups worked the fields and their trades. The elders always had a place of honor in the home. In our modern, mobile, splintered society, both child care and elder care have become out of control and disorienting in their separation from the life of families.

The future numbers of an aging population seem to be astoundingly large. The growing dissatisfaction with the quality of care for the aging has already begun a revolution in the field. The dysfunction of the health care system for all of our society needs to be addressed in the near future. The loneliness and the alienation of the lives of elders make no sense. There have to be better ways.

ACCEPTING NEW INNOVATIONS AND STRATEGIES

The next generation of care will be determined by some of the best minds working today. New technologies have begun to be developed in adaptive equipment to make life easier. The Age Lab at the Massachusetts Institute of Technology describes a new growth market in our economy as being for the old-age generation. At the turn of the twentieth century, the fastest growing age group was teens, whereas at the turn of the twenty-first century, the fastest growing age group was those who are eighty-five and older. The engineering of products from automobiles to can openers aims to make life more comfortable and accessible for seniors.

The American Seniors Housing Association, an organization formed in 1991, has grown to represent 350 companies that own or manage more than a half million housing units. Their facilities range from independent living to senior apartments, assisted living, and continuing care retirement facilities. As part of their comprehensive wellness initiatives, they have begun to utilize computerized brain fitness centers in their facilities. These regimens may indeed be helpful in stimulating brain activity. Some experts believe that socializing by joining a book club or playing an instrument in the community orchestra might have the same positive effect. All agree that inactivity has a negative effect.

Brain and memory specialists have been developing tools to diagnose dementia at the early stages when elders are exhibiting only mild cognitive impairments. Two different memory tests are now used more often in diagnosis, the Mini Mental State Exam (MMSE) and the more comprehensive Montreal Cognitive Assessment (MoCA). Both may be administered by family practitioners and allow for early intervention of patients with dementias. Since less than 20 percent of patients with dementia are currently diagnosed by their own doctors, the ramifications of these developments could have astounding impact. It is said that fifteen million of the baby-boomer generation will develop some kind of advanced dementia. Alzheimer's disease is just one of them, accounting for less than half of the dementia experienced by the elder population. Early detection means more effective treatments.

The advancements in medical breakthroughs about the way drugs can affect degenerative brain diseases like Alzheimer's is in a growth curve of discovery. One recent development is the Geriatric Depression Scale to separate the overlapping issues of depression and dementia.

The costs of geriatric care vary greatly depending upon the decades of health care that precede old age. Exercise, diet, stress and depression management, and alcohol-consumption moderation prolong healthy life. Cardiovascular disease and type II diabetes are both preventable in most cases.

DISCOVERING THE GREEN HOUSE PROJECT

Models for intentional communities began sprouting up with the work of Dr. William Thomas, a Harvard-educated physician who has dedicated his career to working with seniors. In the 1990s, the Eden Alternative changed the culture of nursing home care to include less regulation and more freedom to include cats, birds, plants, and other living creatures.

Thomas's recent effort, The Green House Project, is a model for residential space affordable for those on Medicaid and Medicare. These architecturally designed homes provide for those who need skilled nursing care and are sized to fit in residential neighborhoods, providing housing for eight to ten people, each having a private bedroom and bath. Easily accessible common spaces include laundry facilities, open kitchen and dining areas, and patios with gardens. There is no institutionalized scheduling, and recreational activities and meal planning are guided by the residents.

The first Green House was built in Tupelo, Mississippi.

The Green House Project is in the process of developing models in all fifty states with grant funding and development loans available through the Robert Wood Johnson Foundation and NCB Capital Impact. Training sites with information and workshops are being established throughout the country.

Different models of intentional communities are being initiated that are designed for multiple generations of residents. Some are based on an agricultural model that includes chickens, goats, beehives, and gardens of commercial produce.

Social networking is a formative influence on the kinds of facilities for seniors in the future. Possibilities are only limited by the imagination, and the baby-boomer generation exhibits promise to deliver unique alternatives. The Internet is buzzing with dreams and plans for the future. It is never too early to begin your own search to plan for the years to come.

Passing

Five years have gone by
since the quiet April Saturday
when my father passed out of this life,
and then out of the kitchen door
of the stately old farmhouse
on a gurney, covered by a sheet.

My brother stood beside me,
beneath an old sugar maple
with just the hint of unfolding
of translucent new leaves,
as a mourning dove softly
cooed in the still air.

The rest of the family sat tucked
starkly in the living room
not able to watch the departing
in their shock and despair;
we, both numb and alert,
carried out our tasks.

My brother saw to the men
and the papers to be signed.
I bundled the medical supplies,
bedding and towels,
hustling them to the car trunk
out of sight, no longer needed.

Grief was submerged below
layers of exhaustion, not gone,
waiting for a time alone
to reach out in blackness,
filling my face and nostrils
seemingly never to retreat.

It spit me out, sometime later,
Completely undigested.

Laurel A. Wicks
Spring 2008

147

Resources

WEB SITES

http://www.aarp.org/research/ageline/

http://www.agesong.com

http://www.changingaging.org

http://www.seniorshousing.org

http://www.sharpbrains.com

http://www.thirdage.com

National Center for Creative Aging

    Web site: www.creativeaging.org

    e-mail: info@creativeaging.org

BOOKS

Chödrön, Pema. *Awakening Loving-Kindness*. Boston:
Shambhala Press, 1996.

Chödrön, Pema. *Comfortable with Uncertainly: 108 Teachings on Cultivating Fearlessness and Compassion.* Boston: Shambhala Press, 2003.

Dennison, Paul E., and Gail E. *Brain Gym: Simple Activities for Whole Brain Learning.* Ventura, CA.: Edu-Kinesthetics, Inc., 1986.

Levine, Carol, ed. *Always on Call: When Illness Turns Families into Caregivers.* Nashville, TN.: Vanderbilt University Press, 2004.

Ruiz, Don Miguel. *The Four Agreements: A Practical Guide to Personal Freedom (A Toltec Wisdom Book).* San Rafael, CA: Amber-Allen Publishing, 2001.

So Far Away: Twenty Questions for Long-Distance Caregiving. Bethesda, MD: National Institute on Aging, a department of the U.S. National Institutes of Health (www.nia.nih.gov).

Medical Centers & Agencies

Soldiers & Sailors Memorial Hospital, Penn Yan, NY

St. John's Medical Center, Jackson, WY
(www.tetonhospital.org)
 Hospice of the Tetons
 Professional Home Care

Yates County Office for the Aging, Penn Yan, NY

NOTES